Portrait of
BRITISH COLUMBIA

by Al Harvey

Altitude Publishing
The Canadian Rockies / Vancouver
www.altitudepublishing.com

British Columbia
is a land of immense
diversity, unparalleled
majesty and vast spaces.

The land stretches from the
lofty Rockies on the eastern
border to the pounding
surf of the Pacific
Ocean.

It is a province of
remote wilderness as well
as urban sophistication.

It is one of the
most beautiful
—and most
haunting—places
on the face of the earth.

PORTRAIT OF BRITISH COLUMBIA

Cataloguing in Publication Data
Harvey, Al, 1944-
Portrait of British Columbia

Hardcover ISBN 1-55153-182-8
Paper cover ISBN 1-55153-219-0
1. British Columbia—Pictorial works. I. Title.
FC3812.H37 2002   971,1'04'0222   C2002-910587-0
F1087.8.H37 2002

We acknowledge the financial support of the Government of Canada through the Book Publishing Industry Development Program (BPIDP) for our publishing activities.

Design: Stephen Hutchings and Scott Manktelow
Production Management: Scott Manktelow
Layout Assistant: Hermien Schuttenbeld

Altitude Publishing Canada Ltd.
The Canadian Rockies / Vancouver
Head office: 1500 Railway Avenue,
Canmore, Alberta T1W 1P6
1-800-957-6888
www.altitudepublishing.com

Front cover: Northwest Nootka Island, off British Columbia's West Coast
Back cover: The Bugaboos
Frontispiece: Mt. Tatlow in the Elkins/Nemiah Valleys
Previous pages: Sunset over the Coast Range northwest of Pemberton
This page: Kelp garden off the Queen Charlotte Islands
Opposite: The Lions over Vancouver

Printed in Canada by Friesen Printers

Altitude GreenTree Program
Altitude will plant two trees for every tree used in the production of this book.

PORTRAIT OF BRITISH COLUMBIA

CONTENTS

THE ISLANDS

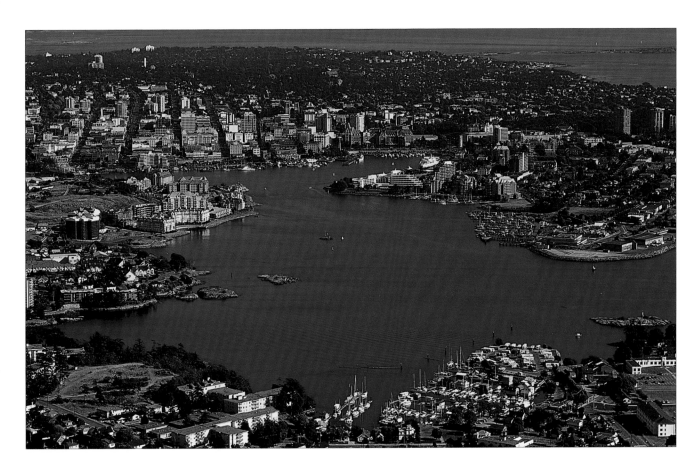

Above The Inner Harbour is the focal point of British Columbia's capital city. Inside the protected harbour the Legislative Buildings and the majestic Empress Hotel are architectural landmarks. Fort Victoria was first settled by Europeans in 1843 and was designated as the colony's capital a quarter century later.

Opposite West Coast beaches, like this one on Whaler Island in Clayoquot Sound, are a great place to find floating treasures from across the ocean.

Running parallel to the southern BC coast, Vancouver Island shelters the mainland from the open Pacific Ocean to the west. Georgia Strait becomes more narrow about halfway up the Island to form Johnstone Strait. A maze of small islands at the mouth of deep coastal inlets meet the north end of the Island.

The Island's spine is the Vancouver Island mountain chain that for much of their length are the division between the rugged and deeply indented west coast and the rain shadow on the east side of the mountains. The Pacific coast is met by a series of inlets and sounds with small islands at their mouths, a paddler's paradise. Expansive sand beaches punctuate the ocean coast, the best known and most accessible of which is Long Beach. The east side of the Island is drier and is the location of the Island highway that runs from south to north. Most of the population resides along this side and enjoys the recreation potential of sheltered islands, beaches, and nearby wilderness.

Above Tourists and residents are equally enthusiastic about Victoria's charms. The architecture alone keeps tourist cameras busy. Much of the architecture is from a century ago, in the heyday of the architect Francis Rattenbury who was most notably responsible for the Legislative Buildings and the Empress Hotel. Every evening over three thousand electric lights outline the seat of the provincial government.

Right Flower baskets by the hundreds adorn the downtown streets of Victoria. The Malahat Building overlooks the harbour and has seen much of Victoria's history.

Above Captain Cook gazes toward the Empress Hotel that he might have seen if only he'd lived another century and a quarter. The Empress Hotel and Victoria itself were both named for the longest reigning monarch in British history. The hotel was completed in 1908 by the Canadian Pacific Railway and is now one of the Fairmont chain of hotels that span the nation.

Left Also completed in 1908 as the fantasy of Robert Dunsmuir, a wealthy industrial-ist, Craigdarroch, or "the castle," is said to be the most expensive private residence ever built in Canada. It has served in several capacities before becoming a museum.

Above A schooner sails by the historic Fisgard Lighthouse near Victoria.

Right An autumn sunset saturates the upper Saanich Peninsula. Off shore are the southern Gulf Islands and the American San Juan Islands with Mount Baker behind. The Saanich Peninsula, north of Victoria, is dotted with acreages and small farms. It is an idyllic area to explore by bicycle. Flower and produce stands abound along the country roads, many with small money boxes supporting the "honour system" of payment.

Opposite A flower basket hangs in front of the provincial Legislative Building.

Above Sand beaches can be found in small coves as well as straight stretches of coastline. This pocket of beach is along the popular West Coast trail. Reservations are necessary for the seven day hike along the coast.

Left Grandfather and grand daughters stroll the pier at Cowichan Bay. The Gulf Islands, blessed with mild winters and an unhurried lifestyle, lie to the southeast of Vancouver Island.

Previous pages The Butchart Gardens, north of Victoria, is the most popular tourist attraction on Vancouver Island.

Above The town of Chemainus faced an uncertain future in the early 1980's with the closing of it's only sawmill. Although another sawmill replaced it, Chemainus embarked on a re-vitalization program that featured historical murals painted on the sides of old buildings throughout the town, drawing streams of curious snapshooting tourists.

Right About 100 kilometers north of Victoria, Cowichan Lake is bathed in sunrise. Formerly home to logging camps and sawmills, the lake now provides wilderness camping and recreational boating.

Above Nanaimo is approximately an hour and a half drive north from Victoria along the east coast. The "Hub City" was founded in 1849 when coal was mined and a Hudson Bay Company fort was established at the Bastion on the waterfront.

Left Maple Bay is sheltered from Georgia Strait by Saltspring Island, the largest of the Gulf Islands. Small bays and coves along the coast are accessed by piers for the local mariners. The climate attracts year-round tourism as well as associated businesses such as Bed and Breakfasts and rural brew pubs.

Above The east coast of Vancouver Island is renowned for its sandy beaches and protected waters. Facing Georgia Strait, Qualicum Beach caters to a brisk tourism trade in the summer months as families flock to the beach community to enjoy the tidal flats and warm water.

Right Orcas, or killer whales, are common in the waters off the coast of Vancouver Island, as well as further north along British Columbia's shores. They are a highly social animal, who live in very complex communities. Some may live as long as 80 years.

Above Tofino, at the north end of Long Beach, is the portal to majestic Clayoquot Sound where islands and inlets provide tranquil refuge from the open ocean. Tofino is a favourite tourist destination. Whale watching is a featured activity.

Right Cathedral Grove is a small stand of old growth forest untouched by logging. Just east of the Alberni Valley, the primeval grove is visited by a quarter million people a year.

Opposite The most popular attraction on BC's Pacific coast is Long Beach where the surf washes an intermittent stretch of sand beaches from Ucluelet to Tofino.

Above The Pacific Ocean reaches Port Alberni via the long Alberni Inlet that stretches northeastward. The local economy has traditionally been based on forestry, the city dominated by a large pulp and paper mill.

Left Coastal cloud fills the low-lying areas close to sea level near Kelsey Bay. Mariners encounter their share of fog and low cloud during otherwise clear weather days in this area. Across Johnstone Strait, the snow-capped mountains of the Coast Range loom on the mainland.

Above Clayoquot Sound has been the focus of environmental protests against clearcut logging of the coastal forests. Accessed from Tofino, Clayoquot Sound offers splendid outdoor recreational opportunity, especially kayak camping on the many beaches of the islands. From this camp-site on Flores Island, kayakers are within a day's paddling of a number of long, pristine sand beaches.

Right A starfish settles into a buffet of barnacles and mus-sels at low tide. The purple starfish is the most common of the 68 starfish species found in BC waters.

Above The southern Gulf Islands offer superb waterfront property and leisurely sailing in protected waters. At a small island near Swartz Bay a schooner lies at anchor and a navigational aid assists the safe passage along a rocky shoreline.

Left A variety of shells lie clustered on a sandy beach in Clayoquot Sound. The clams, mussels, and oysters provide easy and delicious fare for those living off the sea. Kayakers are wary of the outbreaks of "red tide" that prohibit the eating of shellfish along the coast whenever a toxic algae proliferation occurs.

Above Sailboats find a late afternoon anchorage on the north side of Saturna Island. The Gulf Islands are a favourite destination for yachts from Vancouver and beyond, crossing Georgia Strait when winds are favorable.

Right Two ferries meet in Active Pass between Galiano and Mayne Islands in the Gulf Islands. BC Ferry Corp is a crown corporation and the third largest ferry system in the world. The large ferries pictured here transport cars and passengers travelling between Vancouver Island and Vancouver on the mainland.

VANCOUVER, COAST & MOUNTAINS

Left Downtown Vancouver is squeezed on a peninsula between the deep water harbour of Burrard Inlet on the north and False Creek on the south. In the distance and to the south of the city, rises the dormant volcano of Mount Baker in the state of Washington.

Above At twilight the lights of Vancouver's west end illustrate the density of this downtown residential area. The Planetarium in the foreground is part of a larger complex that includes museums and the Heritage Harbour—a sheltered moorage for historic coastal vessels.

More than half of BC's population lives in the southwest corner of the province, a compact area that includes Greater Vancouver, the lower mainland and Whistler, the Sunshine Coast and the lower Fraser Valley. This valley, which extends eastward for over 150 kilometers from Vancouver, is primarily an agricultural area. Recently, however, urbanization has started to spread across the prime farmland of the valley.

Another area of significant growth in the past few decades has been the Howe Sound-to-Pemberton corridor that includes the resort town of Whistler. The Sunshine Coast north of Vancouver extends up the east side of Georgia Strait to Desolation Sound, a prime destination for sailors.

As elsewhere along the BC coast, the Coast Range is a constant backdrop of imposing peaks. The geography is defined by the mountains, the coastal inlets, and the mighty Fraser River, the floodplain of which provides the only generous portion of flat and arable land.

Vancouver, unlike
any other major North
American city, sits at the
edge of a vast wilderness
frontier. The gentle slopes and
modest peaks to the north of the
city soon break into a wave of rugged
mountains and primeval forests that
stretch all the way to the Arctic. This is seri-
ous wilderness—a place of high risk and immi-
nent danger—and it lies just moments away from
the downtown core of high rise and traffic jam.

Above The totem poles at Brockton Point in Stanley Park are one of Vancouver's most popular tourist sights. Traditionally, totem poles are a carved documentation of family history and status.

Left The Museum of Anthropology at the University of BC houses a trove of First Nation's art and culture. The Museum was designed by renowned architect, Arthur Erickson, whose other projects around the city include Simon Fraser University, the Law Courts, and Robson Square.

Opposite Capilano Suspension Bridge hangs over the Capilano River in North Vancouver.

Above Science World is a remnant of the international exposition that ringed False Creek in 1986.

Right Kitsilano Pool and Kitsilano Beach are popular summertime places. The pool contains heated sea water from May to September.

Opposite top A cruise liner berths at Canada Place.

Opposite left After a stop at Granville Island, a sailboat casts off at False Creek for a day of sailing in the outer harbour.

Opposite right The Skyride gondola lifts tourists and skiers to the top of Grouse Mountain.

Above Day hikers pause beside a mountain pond on Whistler Mountain. The ski chairlifts run all year for the benefit of hikers and mountain bikers in the summer.

Right A couple canoes along the River of Golden Dreams just outside the town of Whistler. The Whistler resort area is an all season destination, whose summer activities rival those of winter.

Opposite The Sunshine Coast, north of Vancouver, contains several lakes tucked into the foothills of the Coast Range mountains. Pictured here is Haslam Lake, just outside the city of Powell River.

Above Fresh snow awaits skiers at Blackcomb Mountain. Many skiers buy a double pass for the day or the season which allows unlimited skiing on either Whistler or Blackcomb mountain.

Right The town of Whistler is lively at any season, catering to the well-heeled tourist as well as the local ski bum. Whistler attracts a very international crowd from the Pacific Rim, Europe, and the United States.

Opposite Ski runs on Blackcomb Mountain. Blackcomb is across a narrow valley from Whistler Mountain, the two mountains being the premier ski destination of North America.

Above The Fraser River narrows to a raging torrent at Hell's Gate in the Fraser Canyon.

Right The Fraser River estuary to the south of Vancouver is a maze of islands and wetlands. On Westham Island, a bird sanctuary welcomes frequent flyers on the Pacific flyway.

Opposite above The Fraser River near Chilliwack.

Opposite left The agricultural Lower Fraser Valley is dominated by nearby Mount Baker.

Opposite right The Vedder Rivera tributary in the Lower Fraser Valley, supports salmon spawning and sport fishing.

Above Alpine meadow wild-flowers erupt in a profusion of colour in Manning Park. About 200 kilometers east of Vancouver, this provincial park is located at the north end of the Cascade Range and is a favorite destination for hiking and skiing.

Left A marshland is cradled in the Coast Range near Hope. The Fraser River leaves the canyon just north of the town, then takes a bend westward where the current slows somewhat on the last 150 kilo-meters towards it's meeting with the Pacific Ocean just to the south of the city of Vancouver.

THOMPSON, OKANAGAN, BC ROCKIES

Above A rocky slope south of Merritt is clad in a mosaic of autumn colour. The Interior enjoys colourful autumns preceding the long winters common to most of Canada.

On the east side of the Coast Range the moderating influence of the ocean has diminished and a Continental climate prevails with cold winters and hot summers. The seasons are more distinct than on the coast where the temperature fluctuations are more modest.

The BC Interior refers to the land east of the Coast Range, the mountains that run the length of the province. Because of the rain-shadowing effect of the mountains, the Interior is generally much drier than the coastal regions which receive the brunt of the moisture blowing in from the Pacific Ocean.

The Fraser River watershed drains much of the BC Interior. In the south lies the Okanagan Valley, well known for it's orchards, vineyards, and recreational amenities. To the east various mountain ranges and lakes define the significant regions such as Shuswap and the Kootenays. East of the upper Columbia Valley and the Rocky Mountain Trench are the Rocky Mountains with their distinctive sandstone strata, the eastern boundary of the province.

The Chilcotin and the Cariboo are east of the Coast Range and straddle the Fraser River. The Chilcotin lies to the west and the Cariboo to the east.

Above Due to the mountainous terrain, the railways follow the Fraser Canyon along an almost impassable stretch of BC's longest river. A train proceeds across this bridge near Boston Bar carrying a load of grain from the Prairies towards storage elevators in Vancouver.

Left Nicola Lake lies just east of the Coast Range. Here the arid landscapes are a dramatic contrast to the rain forests of the coast. This ranching country extends north to the Cariboo, an area of pine forests, lakes and open range.

Above The Thompson River is the main tributary of the Fraser River with their confluence at the town of Lytton. The transcontinental railway follows the river through a spectacular canyon which is popular for white water rafting. A train travels eastward with empty grain cars deadheading the long haul back to the Canadian prairies.

Right: The Fraser River is the conduit for five species of migrating salmon. Spawning salmon finish their life cycle where they started and die shortly after spawning. On their long journeys up the rivers to the spawning grounds they refrain from eating after leaving the salt water.

Above left A cyclist rides across an old trestle from the abandoned Kettle Valley Railway near Kelowna. The railway was one of several lines that crossed southern BC to link to the port of Vancouver.

Above right The Okanagan Valley is known for it's orchards that produce a variety of tree fruits. Apples are the most valuable edible cash crop grown in the province.

Left The Okanagan River connects a string of lakes, including Vaseux Lake, an important bird sanctuary. The valley is carpeted with orchards and vineyards from the Shuswap south to the American border.

Above A narrow isthmus separates Kalamalka and Woods Lakes at the village of Oyama. The "lake of many colours" in the foreground is a very deep lake surrounded by orchards. Rattlesnake Point at the north end of Kalamalka Lake is known for it's thriving population of the endangered western rattlesnake.

Right At the north end of 128 kilometer long Okanagan Lake a community of hives houses honeybees that pollinate the abundant nearby fruit trees, also gathering nectar from alfalfa, clover, and sagebrush. At roadside fruit stands throughout the Okanagan, locally-produced honey is sold with seasonal fruits.

Above At the far south of the Okanagan Valley is the town of Osoyoos, very near the American border. Extensive irrigation transforms the desert landscape into productive orchards and vineyards.

Right The Old Grist Mill is a historic attraction near Keremeos in the Similkameen Valley. Flowers, vegetables, and grain are grown in spite of the arid climate.

Opposite About halfway along Okanagan Lake is the city of Kelowna, the focal point of the Okanagan Valley. The lakefront features ample parkland, hotels, a marina, a waterpark, and a popular promenade.

Above The Monashee Mountains are the backdrop for Christina Lake, one of the warmest lakes in the province.

Left The Slocan Valley in the western Kootenays is rich with mining and forestry history.

Opposite above Nelson, on the western arm of Kootenay Lake, boasts over 300 heritage buildings.

Opposite left The Columbia River flows past Trail, home of the world's largest lead and zinc refiner.

Opposite right A mural adorns a downtown street in the town of Creston.

Above Shuswap Lake lies east of the Thompson Valley and north of the Okanagan Valley. The lake is comprised of four long arms, much of which is only accessible by boat. Remote beaches are visited in the summer months by the many flat-bottomed, rented houseboats that ply the lake and beach themselves at night on the sandy shores.

Left Kamloops, at the confluence of the North and South Thompson rivers, is the commercial centre of the south central interior. Traditionally a ranching area on the southern fringe of the Cariboo, Kamloops is also supported by forestry and mining.

Above Adams Lake is a 65 kilometer long northern off-shoot of Shuswap Lake. The area has been economically sustained by logging during the past century and is enjoyed as a recreational area with a number of cottages and resorts lining the shores.

Right Sockeye salmon with their unmistakable crimson spawning colour gather in the gravel shallows of the Adams River, which flows south from Adams Lake into the Thompson/Fraser watershed. The spawning spectacle peaks every four years with almost two million salmon congregating here to spawn and die, leaving a rich source of carrion for scavengers.

Above The Bugaboos are a group of steep granite peaks at the north end of the Purcell Mountains to the west of the Rocky Mountain Trench. The small grouping of peaks is internationally known for both skiing and mountaineering.

Left Rocky Mountain bighorn sheep graze on a slope in Kootenay National Park. These are one of four types of mountain sheep in the province.

Opposite An alpine glacier spills into a glacial pond in the Bugaboos. These ponds are frequently coloured green or turquoise due to the very fine glacial silt that is ground out of the rock by the advancing ice and is suspended in the water.

Above Clouds hover in the valley below the colourful alpine meadows of Mount Revelstoke National Park.

Left A few kilometers north of Revelstoke is the Revelstoke Dam, one of the highest concrete dams in Canada.

Opposite top Columbia Lake is the source of the 2000 kilometer-long Columbia River.

Opposite left Fort Steele is a fascinating heritage park in the east Kootenays.

Opposite right Golfers enjoy a Rocky Mountain backdrop at Fairmont Hot Springs in the Columbia Valley.

Above Mount Assiniboine, the third highest peak in the BC Rockies at 3618 meters, lies on the Continental Divide which forms much of the boundary between BC and Alberta. The crest of the Rocky Mountains form the border separating the province from Alberta and the rest of Canada.

Left Takakkaw Falls in Yoho National Park is the second highest waterfall in both BC and Canada at 254 meters. Along with many other Rocky Mountain highlights, it became accessible to the public with the completion of the transcontinental railway in 1885.

Above Emerald Lake is recognized by a generation of Canadians as the illustration on the back of the ten dollar bill that was in circulation from 1954 to 1971. Located in Yoho National Park the lake is known for its rich glacial colour.

Right Mount Robson is the highest mountain in the Canadian Rockies at 3954 meters and is the centrepiece of Mount Robson Provincial Park. The park is one of the first in the province and is the source of the Fraser River, the longest river in BC.

CARIBOO, CHILCOTIN, COAST & NORTHERN BC

Opposite Toad Valley south of Muncho Lake is at the northern end of the Rocky Mountains in the northeast corner of the province. Here the rivers drain to the Arctic Ocean in the north.

Above The Alaska Highway attracts a steady parade of campers and RVs along it's journey from Dawson Creek to Fairbanks, Alaska. These RVs travel along one of the most scenic stretches of the highway at the north end of the Rockies, south of Muncho Lake.

Northern B.C. was almost inaccessible by road until the Second World War. After the Japanese invasion of Pearl Harbour, the Americans built the 2450 kilometer long Alaska Highway from Dawson Creek to Fairbanks, Alaska for security purposes. Later, they sold the Canadian portion to Canada for 120 million dollars. The other road access to the north is the Stewart Cassiar Highway.

The northern region of British Columbia is an area of immense landscapes and few people, a vast wilderness stretching between the Coast Range and the Rockies. The economy of the northeast is dominated by oil and gas exploration and production, as well as by farming in the Peace River Valley, an extension of the grain belt of the Canadian prairies. In the west, swift rivers slice through the Coast Range on their way to the ocean, many of them disgorging in the Alaska Panhandle. Some small towns such as Stewart and Atlin are the historical remnants of much larger settlements from a century ago.

The Queen Charlotte Islands, also known as Haida Gwaii, are the northernmost islands and home to a remarkably rich native culture.

Above Alpine meadows bloom near Tatlatui Park in the Omineca Mountains north of Smithers.

Left Smithers is the dominant settlement in the Bulkley Valley, an area economically supported by forestry and the many recreational outdoor activities.

Bottom left Fort St. James National Historic Park depicts life from a century ago. European settlement here goes back to the fur trading post established in 1806.

Bottom right The Huble Homestead, a heritage park north of Prince George.

Opposite top The tranquility of Lindeman Lake at sunrise. The lake is on the historic Chilkoot Trail, the gateway to the famous Klondike gold fields of more than a century ago.

Opposite left The surreal landscape of Nisga'a Memorial Lava Bed Provincial Park was formed in the early 18th century from a volcanic eruption and subsequent lava flow that destroyed two Nisga'a villages and diverted the flow of the Nass River.

Opposite right Traditional houses and totem poles of the Gitksan people were developed as a historic reconstruction of a Gitksan village and opened to the public in 1970 near the town of Hazelton.

Above The Tatshenshini River in the far northwest of the province is the main tributary to the Alsek River which flows through the St. Elias Mountains before emptying at Dry Bay in Alaska. The area became a provincial park prior to being designated as a World Heritage Site in 1994. The Tatshenshini is a favourite of white water rafters because of its remote wilderness, wildlife, and mountain beauty.

Left The sternwheeler "Tarahne" rests on the shore of Atlin Lake at the town of Atlin. The sternwheeler plied the waters of BC's largest natural lake from 1917 to 1936 to serve both miners and outdoor adventurers.

Above A fly fisherman tries his luck at the confluence of the Bulkley and Skeena rivers, near Hazelton. Salmon swim up the rivers as they return from the ocean to their birthplace to spawn in the late summer and early autumn.

Right In the Khutzeymateen Valley, a juvenile grizzly bear gorges on a steady diet of sedge grass after emerging from winter hibernation. During the late summer he will fatten up by feasting on the spawning salmon. Recently, links have been discovered between bears, salmon and the health and bio-diversity of the forest..

Above Many long fjords, reminders of the province's recent geo-climatic history, indent the BC coast. This fiord is at at Rivers Inlet.

Right A totem pole stands a solitary vigil at Bella Coola.

Opposite top The moon rises over Windy Bay Creek estuary in Gwaii Haanas in southern Haida Gwaii.

Opposite left Steller sea lions bark their displeasure at the intruding kayak. Male Stellers often weigh over a ton, almost twice as heavy as a large grizzly bear.

Opposite right Old growth rainforest in Haida Gwaii.

ABOUT THE PHOTOGRAPHER

Al Harvey was born and raised in Vancouver and has lived in this fair city ever since. Over the past three decades he has travelled the province, the country, and the world as a stock photographer, documenting the sights and the natural phenomena with his 35mm camera. His photographic work now comprises almost half a million slides which he archives in his own stock library, *The Slide Farm*. There are currently 20,000 images available for viewing online at www.slidefarm.com.

Al is active in many outdoor pursuits, including extensive backpacking and kayaking trips. His ocean kayaking expeditions have taken him along many hundreds of kilometers of west coast wilderness. Al is also known for his home-made beer which he finds time to brew between photographic adventures.

photo courtesy of *The Kid*